To:

_____

From:

_____

Date:

_____

Message from the Artist/Doodler

Doodling is one of my favorite things to do. I've been doing it since I was a little kid. I can remember going to church with my grandma, and she would always find a scrap piece of paper in her purse for me to draw on. Even today, I still doodle in church. Doodles are a great way to calm down while I think and listen to the world around me.

This Doodle Journal is a collection of great doodle prompts with a devotion for each one. No two are the same and there's no wrong way to doodle, so don't be afraid to start. Keep the devotion in mind as you doodle and think about all the good that God brings you every day.

-Jon Huckeby

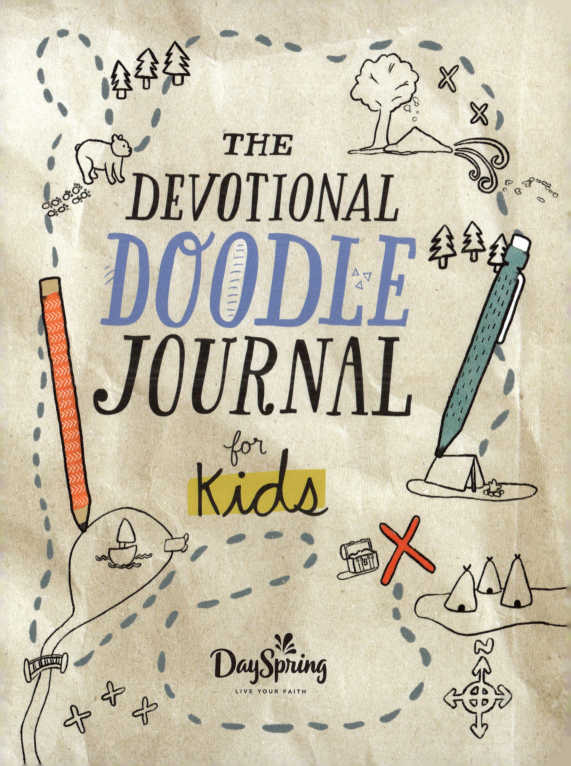

EMOJIS

Aren't emojis fun?!!!? They are always fun to add to a message. They help you express your feelings at the time. ☺ And you know what? God loves for us to express our feelings to Him too. It doesn't matter if we're in a "happy face" mood or it's a "frowny face" day. He knows exactly how you're feeling and He can handle it. He loves to hear from us no matter how we're feeling! Take some time to chat with Him today...you may even think about what kind of emoji you would send Him.

I will forget my complaint,
change my expression, and smile.
JOB 9:27 CSB

Draw in the faces, shapes,
and patterns on the emojis.

NOAH'S ARK

Noah had a lot of faith and trust in God. He believed that God had told him to build the ark...a boat bigger than anyone had ever seen before! Don't you know people teased Noah all the time about it. "God told you to do what?" "Well, that's the dumbest thing I've ever heard of!" Yet Noah kept building. Bible teachers think it may have taken 50-75 years to build. That's a long time to be teased. But God helped Noah stay strong and he finished the ark. Noah is mentioned in Hebrews 11 as one of the heroes of the faith.

It was by faith that Noah built a large boat to save his family from the flood. He obeyed God, who warned him about things that had never happened before.

HEBREWS 11:7 NLT

COAT OF MANY COLORS

Joseph was the second youngest of 12 boys. His father really loved him and made him a beautiful coat of many colors. This made his older brothers jealous. They dug a pit and threw Joseph in it. They then sold Joseph to be a slave. They took his coat and put blood on it and took it back to their father and said Joseph had been killed. But God had other plans for Joseph. He became Pharaoh's right hand man. And when there wasn't enough food for all the people in the land, he stored a lot of it and helped people survive. Joseph's brothers came and asked for food. They didn't know it was Joseph. Joseph had them bring their father back and then Joseph gave them all food and told them who he was. Joseph forgave his brothers and his dad was very, very happy to see that Joseph was alive! Can you imagine forgiving someone who sold you as a slave? Is there someone you need to forgive today?

Jacob loved Joseph more than he did any of his other
sons, because Joseph was born after Jacob was very
old. Jacob had given Joseph a fancy coat.
GENESIS 37:3 CEV

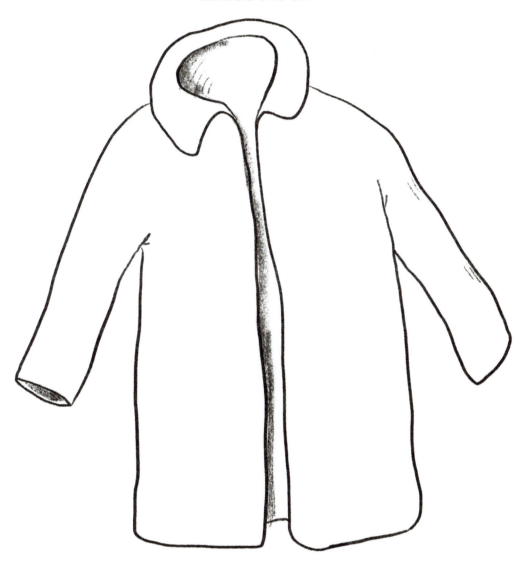

Color the coat of many colors!

QUEEN ESTHER

Did you ever get the feeling that you were at the right place at just the right time? Well, that's the way Queen Esther was. She became queen at a time when a bad man decided it would be a good thing to kill all her people, the Jews. Queen Esther's Uncle Mordecai made her aware of what was happening. She boldly went to the King and told him about the evil plot. She ended up saving all her people. She was definitely made Queen "for such a time as this." God has you where you are for a reason too!

Maybe you were made...
for just such a time as this.
ESTHER 4:14 The Message

Draw crowns, tiaras, jewels,
and finish drawing the palace.

There's a story in the Bible about people bringing kids to Jesus. His disciples were sending them away but Jesus told them to "Let the kids come to Me!" You know why? Because Jesus loves kids! He wanted to bless them. Young kids, older kids, red, yellow, black, brown, and white kids, short kids, tall kids...Jesus loves them all. Do you ever feel like you're too young to be noticed by Jesus? Well that's definitely not true. He loves you and wants to be your friend!

Jesus said, "Let the children come to Me, and don't try to stop them! People who are like these children belong to God's kingdom."

MATTHEW 19:14 CEV

Fill in the faces of the kids. Make them all look different.

CALL ME

We have a "direct line" to the King of kings and the Lord of lords, the awesome Most High God, Creator of the universe. And you know what? He loves for us to call on Him...He answers us every time. We may not always receive the answers we want, but we can always have hope, knowing that God knows more than we do. He is working all things together for our good, and the amazing part is: we can talk to Him about these things anytime we want.

Call to Me and I will answer you and tell you great
and incomprehensible things you do not know.

JEREMIAH 33:3 CSB

Design some cell phone covers.

GOOD DAY'S WORK!

The third day of creation was a busy day for God. Genesis 1:9-13 tells us that God gathered the water together in one place, let dry ground appear, plants, trees and all other vegetation. Not a bad day's work! But how did He do it? How did He gather the waters together? How did He create all of the types of plants in one day? He is incredibly awesome! Isaiah 40:12 says that God measured the waters in the hollow of His hand. God is amazing...and He knows a lot about getting things done!

Draw and color different kinds
of trees and plants.
Feel free to make them up.

Have you ever taken the time to lie down outside at night and gaze up at the heavens? God has created planets, moons, and stars for us to enjoy with our eyes.
Scientists now estimate that there are as many stars in the sky as there are grains of sand on all of the beaches in the world! One handful of sand is estimated to have about 10,000 grains. This means there are trillions upon trillions of stars out there! He even has a name for each of them! God is so powerful!

He counts the stars and calls them all by name.
PSALM 147:4 NLT

CRAZY IN LOVE

Our God is crazy in love with us! Isn't it amazing that He even thinks about us? Think about it, the God who created the entire universe, who spoke worlds, stars, fish, and all the animals into existence thinks about us, cares for us, and loves us! What an awesome God He is!

Color, draw, or doodle in the details to the planets.

Even before He made the world,
God loved us and chose us in Christ
to be holy and without fault in His eyes.
EPHESIANS 1:4 NLT

LIKE A SEED

Every person on the planet is kind of like a seed. A potential-packed package that needs the right environment to grow into a vibrant, green, leafy masterpiece. While seeds need sunlight, water, and soil to grow into full-blown plants, people need encouragement, love, support, and hope in their almighty Father to grow in their faith journey. They weather the winters, suck up the springtime rain, share fruit in the summer, and lose leaves in the fall. These seed-people have discovered that the Master Gardener knows what He's doing. And for that they will bear fruit the rest of their lives.

For you were continually straying like sheep, but now you have returned to the Shepherd and Guardian of your souls.

I PETER 2:25 NASB

Think about the undersea world of God. Sea horses, octopuses, whales, sharks, sawfish, eels, starfish—what an incredible fantasy world that God made real. What about the variety of insects and bugs He made? Crickets, spiders, June bugs, walking sticks, ticks, and chiggers are just a few of the millions of the intricately designed array of insects. Some are so small they are hard to detect with the human eye, yet God handcrafted each one. God has created flowers of every size and color imaginable for our enjoyment. Trees that reach to the sky, waving to their Creator in the breezes, are made for us to lie under and marvel at their greatness. God is incredible!

Glorify the LORD with me, and let us
praise His name together.
PSALM 34:3 NCV

CRAZY ABOUT YOU

God loves you. He's crazy about you. He's your biggest cheerleader. His plans for you are good, and He has a wonderful purpose for your life. He thinks about you more than you think about yourself. Not only does He know how many hairs you have on your head, but He knows how many you lost this morning while brushing it! God thinks you're so special that He didn't make anyone else just like you. You are His unique creation, and He likes what He created in you! Our awesome God cares about the smallest details in your life.

God, Your thoughts are precious to me. They are so many! If I could count them, they would be more than all the grains of sand.
PSALM 139:17, 18 NCV

Now, you can be a hairstylist and show off your creative genius.

Is that amazing or what?!! The King of kings, Lord of lords, great I AM, Bright and Morning Star, Alpha and Omega, Prince of Peace...hears YOU! What a privilege and honor to be able to have a conversation with Him!

And this is the boldness we have in God's presence: that if we ask God for anything that agrees with what He wants, He hears us.

I JOHN 5:14 NCV

What messages would you text God? Write them in.

Isn't it great to know God has good plans for us? It would be disturbing to hear "My plans for you are to have a terrible life yet make it to heaven by the skin of your teeth." While we know life is not a bed of roses and we'll all face difficult times, we can also be assured that His plans for us are good.

"For I know the plans I have for you," says the LORD.
"They are plans for good and not for disaster,
to give you a future and a hope."
JEREMIAH 29:11 NLT

Complete the flower beds.
Add more flowers and color.

HOME SWEET HOME

God, in His infinite wisdom, created the family structure. He knew we would need a support base, close people to laugh, share, eat, and even cry with. The old adage, "There's no place like home" is very true, but this truth is even more powerful for a Christian. Our true home, our heavenly home, is unimaginable in its splendor. Leave it to our Big God to create a city with golden streets, crystal seas, gates of pearl, and even a mansion prepared for you! But most of all, we'll get to laugh, eat, share, and spend time with Jesus!

There are many rooms in My Father's house; I would not tell you this if it were not true. I am going there to prepare a place for you. After I go and prepare a place for you, I will come back and take you to be with Me so that you may be where I am.
JOHN 14:2-3 NCV

Finish adding the details to these houses. Think windows, siding, bricks, chimneys, solar panels, rock, shutters, shingles, shrubs, etc.

MOST EXCELLENT

In the beginning, God created the heavens and the earth.
He made the light, and it was good. He then made strawberries,
the stars and the moon, green grass, giant mountains and,
oh yes, human beings too. And it was all very good.

His radiance exceeds anything
in earth and sky;
He's built a monument—
His very own people!
PSALM 148:13, 14 The Message

When the time was right, the sea parted, the walls fell down, the lions went hungry, the sun stood still, the waves were calm, the stone was rolled away, the clouds were parted, the Lord ascended. And when the time is right, the King of kings will return. God is never early and He's never late— He's always right on time and His plan for you is good.

So let's not get tired
of doing what is good.
At just the right
time we will reap a
harvest of blessing if
we don't give up.
GALATIANS 6:9 NLT

Fill the insides of these clocks
with things the Lord has been
right on time with in your life.

PRAYER ASSIGNMENTS

Ever feel like you're supposed to be praying for something big... something way out there? Sometimes we feel compelled to pray for people we've never met, circumstances we've never faced, and foreign lands we've never visited. This is what some call a "prayer burden." God places compassions on our hearts, and calls us to pray for His people and kingdom. A prayer burden is usually an unselfish concern and a personal assignment. Are you willing to take an assignment? Maybe it's time to let Him know you're willing and able to pray for anything on His agenda today.

God sent His Son into the world not to judge the
world, but to save the world through Him.
JOHN 3:17 NLT

Add more roads, trees, and
houses to finish making the map.

ONE-OF-A-KIND

There are over 7 billion people on planet earth today. It's nearly unfathomable to imagine, but not one of them is alike. Each person is a unique, one-of-a-kind creation, handcrafted by the very hands of God. No one looks alike, talks alike, smiles or laughs alike. Look at your thumbprint. God is so into details that He even individually hand-carved a unique thumbprint for each person. Why did He do that? God is just incredibly into details! He regards each person as a mother regards a newborn baby. He's incredibly proud of each one and head-over-heels in love with His children!

Thank You for making me so wonderfully complex!
Your workmanship is marvelous—and how well I know it.
PSALM 139:14 NLT

Finish adding all the details to the heads here. Get creative!

"If you remain in Me and My words remain in you, then you will ask for anything you wish, and you shall have it." JOHN 15:7 GNT

Really? Does Scripture really say that we can ask for anything and have it? Sure it does...but Scripture also explains that statement. It says *"if"* you remain in Christ, *"then"* you may ask for anything. So what does it mean to *"remain in Him?"* Are you surrendering yourself to His will on an hourly basis? Just imagine what it would be like to totally believe, trust, savor, rest, and receive Jesus every minute of every day.

Those who remain in Me, and I in them, will produce much fruit.
JOHN 15:5 NLT

BIRDS EYE VIEW

Have you ever stopped to think just how many birds exist in the world today? A quick internet search estimates there are 200- to 400-BILLION. Just think about it—if there are over seven billion people in the world, then that would mean there are 30 to 60 birds per person. And God makes each one of them unique—each wing, beak, feather—all different and beautiful in its own way. Isn't God amazing?

Look at the birds. They don't plant or harvest or store food in barns, for your heavenly Father feeds them. And aren't you far more valuable to Him than they are?

MATTHEW 6:26 NLT

Quack!

Turn these blobs into birds.

FOG BE GONE!

George Mueller was a prayer warrior. He was traveling on a ship across the ocean when a great fog descended. After the ship's captain told him it would be impossible to make it to his meeting in time, Mueller asked the captain if they could go inside to pray. Mueller prayed and told the ship's captain that the fog would be gone when they returned to the deck...and it was! The ship's captain was amazed and went on to tell numerous people about it in voyages to come! They also made it to Mueller's meeting on time. Have you seen God do amazing things as the result of your prayers? Maybe it's time to recount His kindnesses to you.

Draw in some boats and ships.

You are the God of great wonders! You demonstrate
Your awesome power among the nations.
PSALM 77:14 NLT

SWEET-SMELLING PRAYERS

Do you have a spot in your home where you store treasured possessions? Perhaps it's a piece of art you created. Maybe it's a birthday card from someone special. Or it could be your grandmother's Bible. Did you know God has a place like that? Do you know what's in it? YOUR PRAYERS! That's right—they are such a treasure to Him that He keeps them in golden bowls. Now that you know your prayers are treasured possessions of God, is there something special you'd like to say to Him?

And when He took the scroll, the four living beings and the twenty-four elders fell down before the Lamb. Each one had a harp, and they held gold bowls filled with incense, which are the prayers of God's people.
REVELATION 5:8 NLT

THANKS AND PRAISE

Each new day is filled with things to be thankful for—from big events such as having another day of life, to small ones such as enjoying a playdate with your best friend. But it's easy to forget to give thanks. Sometimes our feelings don't lend to thoughts of gratefulness—it's much easier to dwell on what is wrong rather than what is right. When that happens, the best cure is to start giving thanks about anything—the key is just to start. Give thanks for the first thing that comes to mind—nothing is too small. All gratefulness builds into a big deposit of love for the One who gives us reason to live and praise His name.

Enter His gates with thanksgiving; go into His courts with
praise. Give thanks to Him and praise His name.
PSALM 100:4 NLT

HE IS FAITHFUL

God's love is before your very eyes. Really, it's all around.
No matter where you are, take a look and start counting His
touches of love. If you're inside, there are walls holding a roof
over your head. Electricity and a place to sit and rest are part of
His provision. If you're outside, you have the warmth of the sun,
birds chirping, and a soft breeze caressing your face. All of these
provisions, plus so many more, are His ways of loving and showing
you He cares about where you are and the details of your life. He
is faithful right before your very eyes, you just have to look.

GOD'S LOVE IS EVERYWHERE

For Your faithful love guides me, and I live by Your truth.

PSALM 26:3 CSB

LET GOD OUT OF HIS BOX

Everyone has their own opinion on who God is and what He does. But there is one thing we know for sure: God is more than any of us can imagine. It's easy to believe that He is too busy to help us with the ins-and-outs of our day-to-day life, but the truth is: God is all-knowing, all-powerful, and He is present everywhere at the same time. He is big enough to take care of the details, big or small. He's definitely greater than any box we may put Him in!

Fill in the boxes with challenges or obstacles in your life that God is bigger than.

How great is our Lord!
His power is absolute!
His understanding is
beyond comprehension!
PSALM 147:5 NLT

PRAYER COVERING

Don't you just love the passage about the armor of God? Because of the gift of His mighty armor, we know that we can walk and live every day within the safety of His full protection. In fact, there may be someone out there that needs to be covered in His armor this very moment. They could be on the other side of the world, next door, or in the other room. Remembering to pray for protection over those in danger could make all the difference.

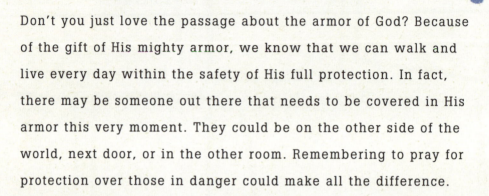

Finally, be strengthened by the Lord and by His vast strength. Put on the full armor of God so that you can stand against the schemes of the devil.
EPHESIANS 6:10-11 CSB

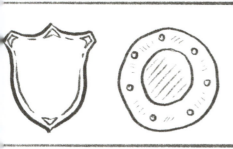

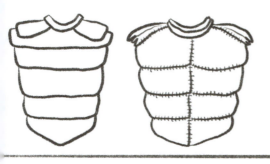

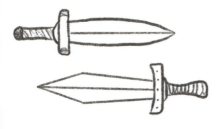

HE REJOICES OVER YOU!

The same God that spoke the world into existence rejoices over you! Is that amazing or what?! You give Him so much joy, in fact, that He starts singing! Yes, He chose you to be in His family, imperfections and all. He chose you for a special purpose. And when you seek Him and carry out that purpose, He has blessings above your imagination in store.

The Lord your God is with you; the mighty One will save you. He will rejoice over you. You will rest in His love; He will sing and be joyful about you.
ZEPHANIAH 3:17 NCV

Music!!!
Fill this page
with as many
musical items
as you can
imagine.
Think notes,
treble clefs,
instruments,
radios, etc.

SCHOOL DAZE!

Some days are harder to get up and go to school than others. Especially after a long summer, Christmas Break, or Spring Break! But you know there are so many great things about school. Besides learning things that will help you the rest of your life, there's all the time you get to hang out with your friends! On those days that you have a big test or it's just a struggle to get up and go to school, ask God to give you the energy, courage, and strength you need to face whatever lies ahead that day. And if you see a friend having a tough day, encourage and help them get through it too.

SCHOOL BUS

STOP

Draw happy faces on the kids on the school bus. Fill the rest of the page with backpacks, notebooks, pencils and school supplies.

Encourage each other daily.
HEBREWS 3:13 CSB

HUSTLE & BUSTLE

Life can get crazy busy. Basically we get up, shower, run out the door to school, hurry home, soccer practice, dinner, homework, veg for a few hours, and go to bed, to repeat it again the next day. Aaaagh!! This crazy cycle can be exhausting. Yet in the midst of this craziness, God says: "Be still and know that I am God." Wait a minute. Screech on the brakes. What did He say??? Be still??!!!!!!! That's right...be still, talk to Him, then listen...listen very intently...and you just might hear that still, small quiet voice speaking to you.

Add details to the city scene below.
We already started a few. Think windows, leaves,
awnings, birds in the sky, people, etc.

Be still, and know that I am God.
PSALM 46:10 KJV

GOD'S HANDS

Do you know the song *He's got the whole world, in His hands...?* When things are running smoothly, it's easy to believe that we are in total control, and ultimately in charge of our lives. But, the truth is, He is in control. He is working in all things, all the time, all around us, everywhere we go. And He is doing it for our good. Isn't that refreshing? Can't you just imagine God's hands holding you? Holding your family? Holding the planet? The entire universe?

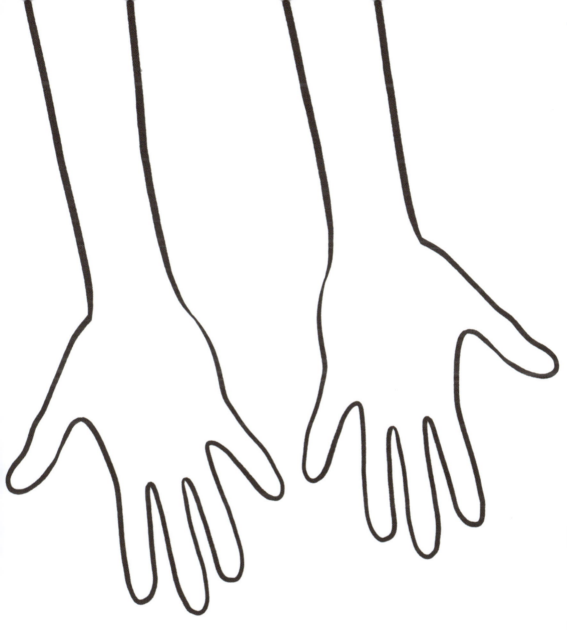

Who else has held the oceans in His hand? Who has measured off the heavens with His fingers? Who else knows the weight of the earth or has weighed the mountains and hills on a scale?
ISAIAH 40:12 NLT

Fill in the hands with the things you'd like God to help you hold. Words or drawings.

SHARK DAY!

Sometimes sharks get a bum rap. After all, sharks were created by God. But what comes to mind when you think of sharks? Yep, your brain starts screaming "Danger! Danger!" While hanging out with sharks may not be the best idea, thinking about them as God's creation kind of puts things in perspective. People are sort of that way too. We all have those people that when they come to mind we hear "Avoid! Avoid!" When this happens, maybe it's a good time to lift up a little prayer and ask God to help us see that person (or shark) through His loving eyes instead of our own flawed vision.

God looked over everything He had made;
it was good, so very good!
GENESIS 1:31 The Message

Doodle in the details to the shark shapes.
Don't forget the gills!

THE CREATOR IS CREATIVE

There are 7.77 million different types of animals in this world. And the Bible says all of them were made in one day. Talk about creativity! God carefully crafted, painted, and designed every creature, from the red-and-black dotted ladybug to the long-necked giraffe, the colorful wings of the butterfly to the stubby legs of the rhinoceros. He created cows to produce milk and chickens to produce eggs. And He breathed life into 7.77 million creatures. In one day. Wow.

Then God said, "Let the earth produce every sort of animal, each producing offspring of the same kind— livestock, small animals that scurry along the ground, and wild animals." And that is what happened.
GENESIS 1:24 NLT

SHINY FISH

Humorist Barbara Johnson once said, "The truth is that even in the midst of trouble, happy moments swim by us every day, like shining fish waiting to be caught." Isn't that true? Life is a series of ups and downs. But even in the hard times, God brings along the giggle of a baby, the song of a bird, or a best friend calling you out of the blue. There are so many things to be thankful for.

Finish drawing and coloring in the fish.
Make some of them extra shiny.

May the LORD bless you
and protect you.
May the LORD smile on you
and be gracious to you.
May the LORD show you His
favor and give you His peace.
NUMBERS 6:24-26 NLT

Robins are inspiring birds. They're inspiring because, in the spring and summer months, whenever it rains, they will sing—in the rain. Hearing their song in the rain is a good reminder to give thanks and praise to God even when it is raining in life. Not only will your own heart be glad, others will take notice and maybe even start singing too. If robins are mindful enough to sing to their Creator while clouds hover and raindrops fall, we can be as well.

Then God said, "Let the waters swarm with fish and other
life. Let the skies be filled with birds of every kind."
GENESIS 1:20 NLT

WALKING ON WATER

The disciples had rowed nearly all night long and were not making much progress in the storm. They had to be worn out! Then all of a sudden they see this creature, or ghost, or, wait... is that Jesus? Scripture says Jesus came to them walking on water and He wanted to walk past the boat. What? Was Jesus racing the boat? Being the sensitive God-man He is, He realized the disciples were afraid of Him. *Don't be afraid guys. It's Me!* And then the crazy thing about this story is that Peter thinks he can walk out into the crashing waves with Jesus...and he does for a while. Jesus gets in the boat and the wind becomes calm. The disciples knew right then, there's something out-of-this-world amazing about Jesus!!

He saw His followers struggling hard to row the boat, because the wind was blowing against them. Between three and six o'clock in the morning, Jesus came to them, walking on the water, and He wanted to walk past the boat.

MARK 6:48 NCV

Add fish and other sea life in the water.

GAMERS

Video games are full of challenges. You either have to overcome obstacles, opponents, or fireball-spitting dragons! It's a challenge to work your way through everything that's thrown at you. In many ways, video games are a lot like real life. There are so many challenges in life. Tests, school, jobs, and at times even people can be challenging. Jesus overcame many obstacles in His life...including the biggest obstacle of all...He even overcame death itself! No matter what life may throw at you, always remember God's got this. He will help you through anything!

I am your God.
I will strengthen you;
I will help you;
I will hold on to you.
ISAIAH 41:10 CSB

Draw your favorite video games
or draw yourself as a video
game character.

THE HUNGRY DRYER

Have you ever put a pair of socks in the laundry basket only to get one of them back? What do you think happens? Maybe the washing machine was hungry and ate it? We've all been there— we're sure we put matching socks in the laundry basket, and now there's one mismatched sock in the clean clothes pile. Usually we give it around six months or so before we finally lose hope and throw it in the trash. Have you ever felt like one of those mismatched socks? Ever feel like you don't seem to fit anywhere the way you should? Don't worry. Remember, God created you one-of-a-kind amazing and He has a special place for you... close to His heart. It doesn't feel fun but hang in there. You'll see His plan for your life come together in His perfect timing.

"For I know the plans I have for you," says the LORD. "They are plans for good and not for disaster, to give you a future and a hope."
JEREMIAH 29:11 NLT

FLOWER POWER

God is the Creator of all the colors in the world. Artists pull inspiration from hues they find in His masterpieces—from the yellow, pink, and orange sunsets to the blue and green ocean and the light brown sand—we create with colors He created for us. And, we've probably only experienced the tip of the iceberg. Many believe there are more colors in heaven—colors we've never seen or could even possibly imagine in our human minds. Amazing, right? Today, let's think about all the colors we get to enjoy on earth, all the different flowers, all the different blooms, every single petal is detailed with amazing, vibrant colors that come from God's breathtaking beauty.

Turn these boxes into flower boxes. Add flowers & then color.

Let's look for wildflowers in bloom, blackberry bushes blossoming white, fruit trees festooned with cascading flowers.
SONG OF SOLOMON 7:12
The Message

WHOOPEE!!!

Isn't it fun to be with a group of family and friends when you hear a funny story and the whole room breaks out into belly laughter? There's no need for the polite little smile, or the fake "ha ha" when you're surrounded by loved ones. In fact, in this space, you are able to completely let loose with uncontrollable laughter, even sometimes to the point of tears. Scripture says we're created in the image and likeness of God. Maybe we don't see a lot of paintings of Jesus laughing or even smiling...but we know He did!!! Won't it be awesome to laugh with Jesus one day?

Finish adding to these happy, laughing faces.

Love from the center of who you are.... Be good friends who love deeply.... Laugh with your happy friends when they're happy.
ROMANS 12:9, 10, 15 The Message

Ever wonder why God made us to require food and water? We sure could save a lot of time, energy, and money if we didn't have to eat or drink. Here's a thought: maybe He knew it would be one of the few times we'd slow down and communicate with one another. We all need loving, caring relationships, and what better way to spur one another along than with a sugar cookie and a chocolate milkshake.

So whether you eat or drink, or whatever you do, do it all for the glory of God.

I CORINTHIANS 10:31 NLT

WALK THIS WAY

When you search online for "How many decisions do we make a day?" you won't find a firm source. However, many articles indicate that the average human makes approximately 35,000 decisions a day. Wow! No wonder we're so ready to go to bed at night. Sometimes don't you wish that God would put road signs in front of us saying "Walk this way!" Scriptures, such as Psalm 37:23, assure us that God is constantly guiding us. And not only does He direct us, He cares about every detail of our lives. Is He awesome, or what?

The steps of the godly are
directed by the LORD.
He delights in every
detail of their lives.
PSALM 37:23 NLT

Create your own shoe tread
patterns on these shapes.

HEADPHONES

Sometimes it's easier to tune people out rather than let them in our world...but God wants us to live in community with others. He also wants us to live in close community with Him. Sometimes we know we are tuning people out, but other times, we may not realize it. And what about God? Do we ever tune Him out? He's the Creator of the Universe and He so longs to hear our voice, to be a part of our lives and to speak to us with His still small voice. Sometimes it's better to tune out the world and tune into Him! He has good things planned for you!

I love the LORD because He has
heard my appeal for mercy.
Because He has turned His ear to me,
I will call out to Him as long as I live.
PSALM 116:1-2 CSB

Draw faces inside all
the headphones.
List below the type
of music or song that
person is listening to!

Sometimes life feels like you're walking through a jungle. You're walking by a beautiful waterfall, enjoying the amazing scenery, when bam...a poisonous snake crosses your path. Immediately the hair on the back of your neck stands up! But you know what? This was no surprise to God. He's got you covered. The snake will soon be gone (one way or the other!) and you'll be back to feeding bananas to the monkeys. Always remember that He will always be with you.

Color the
Jungle!

I am with
you always.
MATTHEW 28:20 CSB

STYLIN'

There are so many cool ways to dress. Fashion really boils down to whatever you like! As you color in all the cool clothes and accessories on the next page, take time to think about the beauty that comes from within you and how that is "precious to God!"

Don't be concerned about the outward beauty of fancy hairstyles, expensive jewelry, or beautiful clothes. You should clothe yourselves instead with the beauty that comes from within, the unfading beauty of a gentle and quiet spirit, which is so precious to God.

1 PETER 3:3-4 NLT

HIDDEN TREASURE

Isn't it fun to think of what it would be like to find a large hidden treasure? Usually, when we think of treasure, we think of a huge room full of gold, diamonds, and jewels of every kind. But in God's Kingdom, there are many other types of treasures. The love of God, the love of your family, a best friend, a cozy place to sleep tonight. There are so many treasures in this world that don't just "sparkle and shine!" Can you think of some treasures in your life that you've been taking for granted? Maybe it's time to thank God for all He has done for you.

Store up for yourselves treasures in heaven. . .
For where your treasure is, there your heart will be also.
MATTHEW 6:20, 21 CSB

START
HERE

Find your way to the treasure chest.
List 5 treasures in your life.

God got pretty creative when He created us. Think about all the different colors of hair. How some are straight, some are curly, and some hair is even missing. Did you know God knows how many individual strands of hair you have on your head? Yep, even after you brush it He knows how many just went away. That's just a glimpse of how much He cares for us and loves us!

Not a single sparrow can fall to the ground
without your Father knowing it.
And the very hairs on your head are all
numbered. So don't be afraid;
you are more valuable to God than a whole flock of sparrows.
MATTHEW 10:29-31 NLT

Fill in the rest of these faces and draw in the hairstyles.

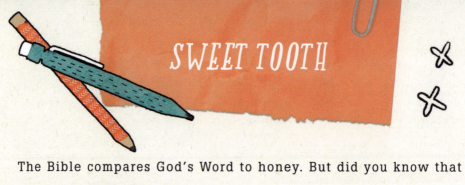

SWEET TOOTH

The Bible compares God's Word to honey. But did you know that during the time the Bible was written, people weren't surrounded with all the sweets available today? Nope. Candy, chocolate, sodas, donuts—none of these existed in those times. In fact, honey was most likely the sweetest thing known to mankind. And, on top of that, it was a rare and precious commodity. What if we treated God's Word like that all the time? What if we craved His Word more than we craved chocolate...or honey?

How sweet Your words taste to me; they are sweeter than honey.

PSALM 119:103 NLT

THE CROSS

The cross is probably the most well-known, recognizable symbol of Christianity today. At one time, it was used as punishment for criminals, yet we wear it around our neck, use it on buildings, and put it on Christian books. Why is it so popular? Maybe it's not the actual cross that is attractive, but the work, the sacrifice, the Man who died on it for our benefit that has made it the symbol it is today. When you get right down to it, it's all about Jesus!

Never boast about anything except the cross
of our Lord Jesus Christ.
GALATIANS 6:14 NLT

Fill this page with crosses.
Big, little, smooth, rugged,
colored, etc. As you do,
think about Jesus and all
He's done for you!

STAINED GLASS

Each individual piece of a stained glass window is really not that pretty by itself. But when you combine all the different colored pieces of glass, it becomes beautiful and has a wonderful story to tell. It's kind of like the Body of Christ. Individually we're uniquely created and loved, but when you combine us all together, we become even more beautiful and are a part of the greatest story ever told.

Design some stained glass windows. Make sure you color them afterward.

We are all one body in Christ, we belong to each other, and each of us needs all the others.
ROMANS 12:5 NLT

HERE KITTY KITTY

There's something calming and soothing about a cat curled up sleeping and purring. It's as if they don't have a care in the world. They've found their "happy place." Our Father likes it when we cast our cares on Him and curl up in His lap and rest. There's no better place to be than spending time with our Heavenly Father.

Apply your special touch to all of these fancy felines.

Give your worries to the LORD, and He will take care of you. He will never let good people down.
PSALM 55:22 NCV

PLANT, WATER, HARVEST

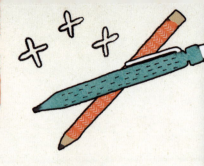

Ever plant a garden? It seems like a long time from when you first plant it until it sprouts out of the ground. And then as you water it, it continues to grow until one day you get a bountiful harvest. That's kind of the way our lives are with God and others. Some people "plant" seeds in our lives, others water, and others harvest...but as the Scripture says, it's God that brings the growth in our lives!

It's not the one who plants or the one who waters
who is at the center of this process but God,
who makes things grow.

I CORINTHIANS 3:7 The Message

Fill this page with veggies.

The discussion God has with Job is classic! God says, "*Who shut the doors to keep the sea in when it broke through and was born, when I made the clouds like a coat for the sea and wrapped it in dark clouds, when I put limits on the sea and put its doors and bars in place, when I said to the sea, 'You may come this far, but no farther; this is where your proud waves must stop'?*" JOB 38:8-11 NCV

Only God Almighty could make the claims He does. Only God can tell the seas, "Your waves can only come this far and then they have to turn around and go back!" His awesomeness is beyond compare, His majesty is unexplainable, His power is limitless!

With a blue or white pen or marker, add wave lines to the water to create patterns. Add some shells or pebbles to the sand.

CAN YOU IMAGINE?

Did you know that there are reportedly 298,000 different types of plant species? And God created them all in one day. It's true! The Bible says He simply said "Let the land sprout with vegetation," and at that very moment plants, trees, grass— every single root that grows from the ground instantly covered the land. Can you imagine? What a sight to watch, as the Great Artist, in all His power filled the dry ground with all different hues of greens, reds, yellows and the many, many different colors God gave us to enjoy. He filled the hills with green pines, the rainforest with banana trees, the deserts with cacti, and the beach with palm trees. He had a purpose for every single beautiful bloom He created—let's remember to praise Him for the beauty He surrounds us with each day.

Doodle some plants & trees
that haven't been discovered yet.
Add some fruits and name them.

Then God said, "Let the land sprout with
vegetation—every sort of seed-bearing plant, and
trees that grow seed-bearing fruit. These seeds will
then produce the kinds of plants and trees from
which they came." And that is what happened.

GENESIS 1:11 NLT

TIME OUT!

Sometimes we just need to call a time out from life. Things can get so busy, and it seems like we just can't keep up. Chores, homework, after-school activities, friendships, church groups... TIME OUT! Jesus knew we'd have times like this. After a busy day of healing, preaching, feeding the 5,000, He would often get away for some one-on-one time with the Father. Time outs are ok!

Redesign the shirts that Refs wear. Come up with your own new colors and patterns.

Crowds of people were coming and going so that Jesus and His followers did not even have time to eat. He said to them, "Come away by yourselves, and we will go to a lonely place to get some rest."
MARK 6:31 NCV

Years ago people used to hang their clothes out on a clothesline to dry. A few brave souls probably still do. The best part about it was that your clothes just always smelled so good! In Scripture we're encouraged to follow Christ and to serve and give to others. When we do this the Bible says it's a pleasing aroma to God. Maybe it even smells fresh and breezy.

Imitate God, therefore, in everything you do, because you are His dear children. Live a life filled with love, following the example of Christ. He loved us and offered Himself as a sacrifice for us, a pleasing aroma to God.

EPHESIANS 5:1-2 NLT

Doodle more clothes on the lines then color them in.

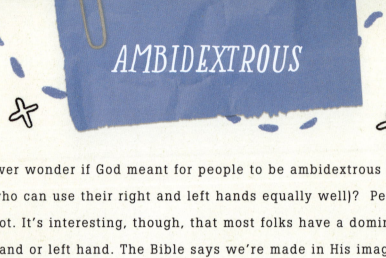

AMBIDEXTROUS

Ever wonder if God meant for people to be ambidextrous (a person who can use their right and left hands equally well)? Perhaps not. It's interesting, though, that most folks have a dominant right hand or left hand. The Bible says we're made in His image and likeness. God has to be ambidextrous! To get everything done that He did during creation...He had to have both hands going at once!!

Left Hand

Right Hand

God created human beings in His image.
In the image of God He created them.
GENESIS 1:27 NCV

BIBLE TRIVIA

Which one of these animals is NOT mentioned in the Bible?

Bat	Lizard	Chameleon	Monkey
Elephant	Dog	Unicorn	Tortoise

Need a clue? Read these verses in your Bible
(or look them up online):

Deuteronomy 14:12,18 KJV   Numbers 23:21-22 KJV

Leviticus 11:29-30 KJV   Judges 7:5 KJV

The Bible is full of interesting details. Have you read
about the sun going backwards? The iron ax head that
"swam?" Or how about the donkey that talked? See if
you can find any of those passages of Scripture!

All Scripture is inspired by God and is profitable for teaching,
for rebuking, for correcting, for training in righteousness.

II TIMOTHY 3:16 CSB

Draw your own version of the animals and color them in.

You know that feeling you get on the last day of school? You know how excited you are that summer break and sleeping in starts TOMORROW?! If you take that feeling and multiply it a million times, you might begin to understand what heaven will be like the first time you see it! The Bible says that for people who love Jesus, He is preparing a place for you that is one-of-a-kind amazing!!!

What God has planned for people who love Him is more than eyes have seen or ears have heard. It has never even entered our minds!

I CORINTHIANS 2:9 CEV

FAMILY TREE

Have you ever thought about praying for your family members? Did your sister have a hard time getting up this morning? Pray and ask God to give her the peace she needs to face the day ahead. Did your brother lose the tournament? Pray and ask God to help lift the disappointment, and let him see all the good that came from playing the game. Does your mom have a cold? Pray and ask God to heal her stuffy nose so that she feels good again. You can always, always lift your loved ones up to God, no matter what they are going through!

Each generation will announce to the next Your wonderful and powerful deeds.
PSALM 145:4 CEV

Fill in your family tree, and as you do, pray for each family member you list.

GOOD FRUIT

God could have made ten different colored apples and been done with it. Surely, ten would have satisfied the human appetite. But God doesn't just satisfy, He goes above and beyond when it comes to expressing His love toward us. He knew we'd love the numerous variety of fruits and the unique tastes from each one. His creativity is breathtaking...His love for us is immeasurable!

But the Holy Spirit produces this kind of fruit in our lives:
love, joy, peace, patience, kindness, goodness, faithfulness.
GALATIANS 5:22 NLT

Don't you just love that God says nothing is impossible for Him? Period. End of discussion. No exceptions. He didn't say, "Well, I can do most things but don't come to me on Tuesdays, Thursdays, or Sundays because I'll probably be napping." No, God tells us that He is on call 24 hours a day, seven days a week and nothing, absolutely nothing is too hard for Him.

I am the LORD, the God of every person on
the earth. Nothing is impossible for Me.
JEREMIAH 32:27 NCV

Doodle impossible things.

KITES

Wouldn't it be nice to be a kite? To fly up into the beautiful blue sky and look down upon the beauty? Wouldn't that be a sight? You could fly high into the clouds, forgetting all your worries and problems. Just floating. Sometimes the winds of life get stormy and it's hard to just let go and let God take care of us. But even in those tough times, God protects us and watches over us. At any moment He can speak "Peace be still" and cause the rough winds to go away. So next time you're trying to solve all your problems on your own, remember you have an almighty God who can take care of things.

Jesus got up and ordered the wind and the waves to be quiet. The wind stopped, and everything was calm.
MARK 4:39 CEV

SIGNS EVERYWHERE!

Jesus speaks a lot about "signs of the times." He indicates that we'll know when His return is soon by different signs on earth. It says no one knows the time but it indicates that we'll know the season. Sounds like a cool time to be alive on planet earth. God's got good things ahead for us!

He told them, "You have a saying that goes, 'Red sky at night, sailor's delight; red sky at morning, sailors take warning.' You find it easy enough to forecast the weather—why can't you read the signs of the times?"

MATTHEW 16:2-3 The Message

Robots come in all shapes and sizes. Some vacuum your floor. Some mow your lawn. Others work on assembly lines to help build cars. There are even some that can talk to you. All robots are programmed to performed a certain job or help with a certain project. In some ways when God created us, He "programmed" us too. And what are we programmed for? To live with Him forever! Once we make the choice to follow His Son Jesus, He has "programmed" us for the great things He has planned for us!

For we are His workmanship, created in Christ
Jesus for good works, which God prepared
ahead of time for us to do.
EPHESIANS 2:10 CSB

Draw
robots!

CREATED TO CREATE

Everyone is creative. Whether you are an accountant organizing spreadsheets, a gardener digging in the dirt, or a brilliant artist painting portraits, you have creative juices running hot through your veins. How do we know this? Because God is the ultimate creator, and He hardwired creativity into our DNA when He made us in His image. Those creative juices you have come straight from Him. Can you imagine Him creating all the animals? From the killer whale and the monarch butterfly to the water buffalo and the tree frog, God created each one unique and beautiful. What creative gifts has God passed on to you? Maybe it's time to stop denying your creative skills and instead, use them to bring glory to the greatest Creator of all.

In the beginning
God created....
GENESIS 1:1 NLT

Buffalo check is a red
and black check pattern.
Add patterns to the other
animals and show what
their check would look like!

DINOSAURS

The word dinosaur actually does not appear in Scripture. Perhaps the words "dragon," or "land monster" refers to what we know as dinosaurs. We do know these huge reptiles lived on our planet and walked this earth and that God obviously created them. But why? And what happened to them? While we don't know for sure, it's amazing to imagine these magnificent creatures roaming the earth. God created a fascinating world, and with it, He continues to remind us of how truly BIG He is—dragons, land monsters, and dinosaurs to humans, cars, and cell phones. He is over all of it.

Everything God created is good.
I TIMOTHY 4:4 The Message

God really spoiled us. Did He really need to create thousands of types of flowers? A simple dozen or hundred would have done. And trees, why so much variety? Ten different kinds could have been enough. And all the clouds? What if just one cloud floated by each day and either it rained or it didn't? He didn't want us to get bored, did He? Take time today to notice all the details He created just for you!

Yes, there will be an abundance of flowers and singing and joy!...
There the LORD will display His glory, the splendor of our God.

ISAIAH 35:2 NLT

AUTOPILOT

On most jets and airplanes the pilot can switch control over to "autopilot," and suddenly the plane is flying itself. That's right, the aircraft has been programmed to steer and completely control the plane without the pilot's assistance. When it's time to land, the pilot simply turns the autopilot feature off and lands the plane. In some ways, God can be like an autopilot feature in our lives. When we give Him control, He will take over and keep you flying smoothly.

God's Spirit makes us loving, happy, peaceful, patient, kind, good, faithful, gentle, and self-controlled.

GALATIANS 5:22, 23 CEV

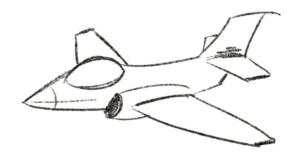

Design your own jets and airplanes.

SPIDER WEBS

Have you ever looked closely at a spider's web...the intricacy, the detail of each little web strand? They can be truly amazing works of art. God imagined this tiny little creature and gave it the ability to capture its food this way. Another example of God's incomprehensible creativity.

The spider skillfully grasps with its hands,
and it is in kings' palaces.
PROVERBS 30:28 NKJV

God gives us so many good things. He fills us with joy and peace. There aren't too many gifts better than those two! God is always going above and beyond any sort of basic creativity. He gives gifts that are better than we need or deserve. What an awesome God He is!

I pray that the God who gives hope will fill you
with much joy and peace while you trust in Him.
Then your hope will overflow by the power of the Holy Spirit.
ROMANS 15:13 NCV

God

Pick out key words
from this verse and
draw and decorate
them on the page.

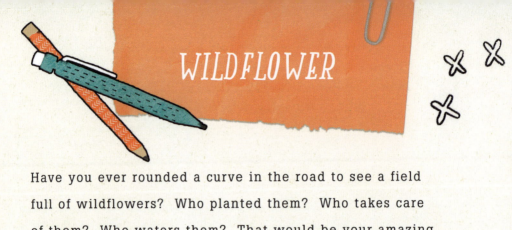

WILDFLOWER

Have you ever rounded a curve in the road to see a field
full of wildflowers? Who planted them? Who takes care
of them? Who waters them? That would be your amazing
heavenly Father who once again loves to surprise you with
His creativity. Remember, He doesn't have to do that. In fact,
another field full of grass would have sufficed, but He goes
above and beyond to share His beauty with us. Thanks, God!

Fill in more
wildflowers in the field.

If God cares so wonderfully
for wildflowers...
He will certainly care for you.
MATTHEW 6:30 NLT

ASK, SEEK, FIND

Scripture says *"Ask, and it will be given to you. Seek, and you will find. Knock, and the door will be opened to you."* (MATTHEW 7:7 CSB) Isn't it nice to know that God promises to give us what we need? He doesn't say "ask, and we might get it." He says "ask, and it will" be given to us. We have a loving Father—One who invites us to lift our wants, cares, and concerns to Him so that He can provide what is best for us. All we have to do is trust.

So I say to you, ask, and it will be given to you. Seek, and you will find. Knock, and the door will be opened to you. For everyone who asks receives, and the one who seeks finds, and to the one who knocks, the door will be opened.
LUKE 11:9-10 CSB

Did you know redwoods are the tallest trees on earth? There are more than 50 redwood trees that have been documented to be at least 360 feet tall. That's the height of a 36-story building! Redwoods can grow to be 8 to 20 feet in diameter, and scientists believe some of them are more than 2,000 years old. Can you imagine standing underneath one of these beautiful, massive, living creations? Take a moment to imagine the wind whistling through its branches as you stand in awe of how powerful and beautiful and big our Creator is.

A God-shaped life is a flourishing tree.
PROVERBS 11:28 The Message

PET ROCKS

Back in the 70s pet rocks were a huge fad. Today many people like to paint faces on rocks. Speaking of rocks, the Bible states that Jesus is our rock. Rocks are strong. Jesus is strong! Lean on Jesus and He will be your rock and will keep you strong!

The LORD is my rock, my
fortress, and my Savior.

PSALM 18:2 NLT

Fill the page with pet rocks.
Name them and describe
their personality.

HOW TO FOLLOW

The Bible has a formula for making your paths go in the right direction. Some people struggle with God's plan for their life. They wonder how they got to where they are, what to do next, and how they should navigate the ups and downs of life. While those are never easy questions, Proverbs does have some direction that may help:

1. Trust God
2. Don't try to figure it out on your own
3. Know and acknowledge God in everything you do
4. God will make your paths straight

Trust in the LORD with all your heart,
and do not rely on your own understanding;
in all your ways know Him,
and He will make your paths straight.
PROVERBS 3:5-6 CSB

Draw anything you want...the only rule is you can only use straight lines on the whole page!

Did you know there are roughly 525 million dogs in the world? There are 340 recognized breeds worldwide, with about half of those living in the United States. The poodle is just one of those breeds. Among poodles, there are three basic sizes:

- Standard
- Miniature
- Toy

The fact that God would create so many different breeds, and then create different sizes of different breeds can only mean that He is a creative God. And, it provides even more evidence of God going above and beyond to bring us more joy.

Finish out
all the
details
on the
doggies.

God richly gives us everything to enjoy.
I TIMOTHY 6:17 NCV

GOD MADE MONSTERS

According to the Bible, God made the sea monster Leviathan to *play* in the ocean. While scholars believe Leviathan might be a crocodile, whale, or maybe even a shark, the point is He created some type of creature to simply *frolic* in the depths of the ocean. God delights in us when we enjoy the beauty that surrounds us. He loves watching life frolic in the goodness that He created. And, just think, if He enjoys watching sea monsters frolic in His creation, how much more does He delight in watching us play around?

Monsters are fun to draw.
Start with a basic shape
then add eyes, mouth, and
all the other parts.
Color all of these when
you're done.

Look at the sea, so big
and wide, with creatures
large and small that
cannot be counted. Ships
travel over the ocean,
and there is the sea
monster Leviathan, which
You made to play there.
PSALM 104:25-26 NCV

HAIR TODAY... GONE TOMORROW

The average lifespan in the United States is approximately 80 years. That's 80 trips around the sun, 29,220 days, 701,280 hours, and 42,076,800 minutes. God encourages us to redeem our time on earth wisely. Life is all about building relationships and glorifying God. Are you sharing God's love with those around you? Are you walking with God in all areas of your life, allowing Him to guide you, and praising Him for the many blessings in your life? Take a moment today to think about where you are in your faith journey, and maybe spend a few of those 42 million-plus minutes to doodle around a little.

But you do not know what will happen
tomorrow! Your life is like a mist.
You can see it for a short time,
but then it goes away.

JAMES 4:14 NCV

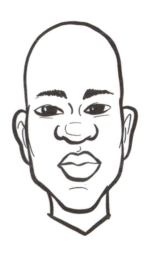

Draw different types of facial hair on these men.
As you do this, think about the men in your life and how you
can build your relationship with them and glorify God.

YOU ARE PRICELESS

When cleaning out a closet or an attic, a lot of time can be spent thinking about whether an item is worth keeping or if it's time to throw it away. The more value or sentimental value the piece has, the better the chance you'll keep it. Otherwise, it goes to the nearest thrift store or the trash. Isn't it wonderful that, when God looks at you, He doesn't compare your worth with someone else's? That's because you are already of the highest quality. To God, you are a keeper...from now to forever.

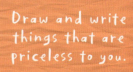

Draw and write things that are priceless to you.

I praise You because You made me in an amazing and wonderful way.
PSALM 139:14 NCV

GOD IS SOVEREIGN

Sovereign is basically a fancy word that means "holds and exercises supreme authority." In other words, God reigns, God rules, and He has the final say. He is ultimately and fully in control of every aspect of our lives. He is all-powerful, He exists everywhere, and He is all-knowing—which means there is nothing, NOTHING, beyond His awareness or ability. Grasp this truth today, and let the peace, rest, and assurance fill your heart, mind, and soul.

Color in however you want.

Get out the message—GOD Rules! He put the world on a firm foundation; He treats everyone fair and square.

PSALM 96:10 The Message

PERSNICKETY

Persnickety. Isn't that just a fun word to say? How about "snickerdoodle" or "kaleidoscope" or "papoose." These words just put a smile on your face. It's as if you can't say them without smiling! There are many people like that in our lives as well—you just can't look at them without getting a smile on your face. It will probably be that way when we see Jesus face to face. We'll probably get the biggest smile on our face and then run into His arms!

Doodle some strange things to go along with some strange and funny-sounding words. Name the two below then create more of your own. Here are a few more words: Bumfuzzle, Snollygoster, Taradiddle, Widdershins, Collywobbles, Gubbins, Xertz, and Bibble.

He and the Lamb will be seated there on their thrones, and its people will worship God and will see Him face to face. God's name will be written on the foreheads of the people.
REVELATION 22:3-4 CEV

No ocean can hold it back.

No river can overtake it.

No whirlwind can go faster.

No army can defeat it.

No law can stop it.

No distance can slow it.

No disease can cripple it.

No force on earth is more powerful

or effective than the power of prayer.

Finish adding color to the planet and the words.
Put an X on the places you want to specifically
pray for. Write your prayers around the earth.

And when he took the scroll, the four living beings and
the twenty-four elders fell down before the Lamb. Each
one had a harp, and they held gold bowls filled with
incense, which are the prayers of God's people.

REVELATION 5:8 NLT

FOUR SEASONS

Winter, spring, summer, and fall...the Lord God designed them all. Would people have even known or cared if it just stayed spring all year? Sure, there are some locations where the weather stays the same year round, but for much of the world, God created the four seasons. Why? We can't say for sure, but maybe because He knew we are created in His image, so He knew we would love the variety as much as He does.

He spreads snow like a white fleece, He scatters frost like ashes, He broadcasts hail like birdseed—who can survive His winter? Then He gives the command and it all melts; He breathes on winter—suddenly it's spring!

PSALM 147:16-18 The Message

One tree, four seasons. Name, color, and add ground details to represent the correct season.

PRIZEWINNER

You can learn a lot about life through sports. Being on a team teaches you how to win and lose gracefully, keep going when the going gets tough, and to keep their eyes on the ball. All of these lessons can prepare you for life as well. The race God has placed in front of you will, no doubt, include winning and losing, getting back up when you fall down, and learning to focus on God during the hard moments. While life is filled with ups and downs, we never know how God is going to use the lessons we learn today to prepare us for what comes tomorrow.

Let us run with endurance the race God
has set before us. We do this by keeping
our eyes on Jesus, the champion who
initiates and perfects our faith.
HEBREWS 12:1, 2 NLT

Fill the page with game
balls. Don't forget to color.

Jesus feeding the 5,000 is quite a miraculous story. It's even more exciting when you take into consideration that there were actually more than 5,000 people. In fact, there were 5,000 men alone. Meaning, if each of these men had a wife and child with them, that's actually 15,000 people that He fed with five loaves of bread and two fish! Not to mention, they had quite a few leftovers. So, next time we start to limit God, let's try to keep this story in mind. Remember, Jesus can take the little we offer up to Him and turn it into enough to meet our needs.

Then Andrew, Simon Peter's brother, spoke up. "There's a young boy here with five barley loaves and two fish. But what good is that with this huge crowd?"

JOHN 6:8-9 NLT

ROSES ARE RED

Roses are such beautiful creations of God. Did you know there are at least 100 species of roses? Did you know some rose blooms are the size of a grain of rice? Roses have been known as a symbol of love. The next time you stop and smell a rose, think about how intricate God designed it and let it remind you of His great love for you!

1. 2. 3. 4.

Here's an easy way to draw a rose. Now, fill this page with roses.

God has made everything beautiful for its own time.
ECCLESIASTES 3:11 NLT

ENCOURAGE ONE ANOTHER!

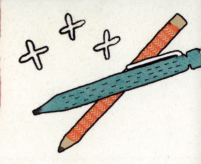

Don't you just love it when someone tells you you're doing a good job? Or compliments you on something you're good at? Or just tells you that you look nice today? These are all different forms of encouragement. Everyone can use encouragement each and every day! Who do you know that could use some encouragement today? Try it out!

CARD LIST

Therefore encourage one another and build each other up as you are already doing.

I THESSALONIANS 5:11 CSB

1.

2.

3.

4.

5.

6.

7.

8.

9.

10.

Make a list of people you've never sent a greeting card to. Start sending out cards to encourage the people on your list!

A LIGHT IN THE DARK

Jesus is the light of the world. He provides protection and guidance by His presence. And, while we may be led into sad places, we have the assurance that we will never be alone. He will always be with us, even when we're sad. What a wonderful feeling it is to know that we will never walk alone in the dark, that the Light of Jesus will always shine inside of us, and that His love for us is stronger than anything we might face!

Jesus spoke to them again: "I am the
ight of the world. Anyone who follows
Me will never walk in the darkness
but will have the light of life."
JOHN 8:12 CSB

Continue drawing the light
bulbs. By each one, write an
idea you have about a way you
can use your creativity for
God's glory.

Z IS FOR ZEBRA

Z is the last letter in the English alphabet. It's the caboose... it's the end. The Bible has a beginning and an end also. One of the names of God is *The Alpha and Omega*...the beginning and the end. The last word in the Bible is "Amen" which basically means "so be it!" So in case you're wondering why you are drawing Zebras around "Amen" we thought it would be a great way to end this book! Be blessed!

Add your kind of stripes or colors to these Zebras!

AMEN!

Jesus, the One who says these things are true, says, "Yes, I am coming soon." Amen. Come, Lord Jesus! The grace of the Lord Jesus be with all. Amen.

REVELATION 22:20-21 NCV

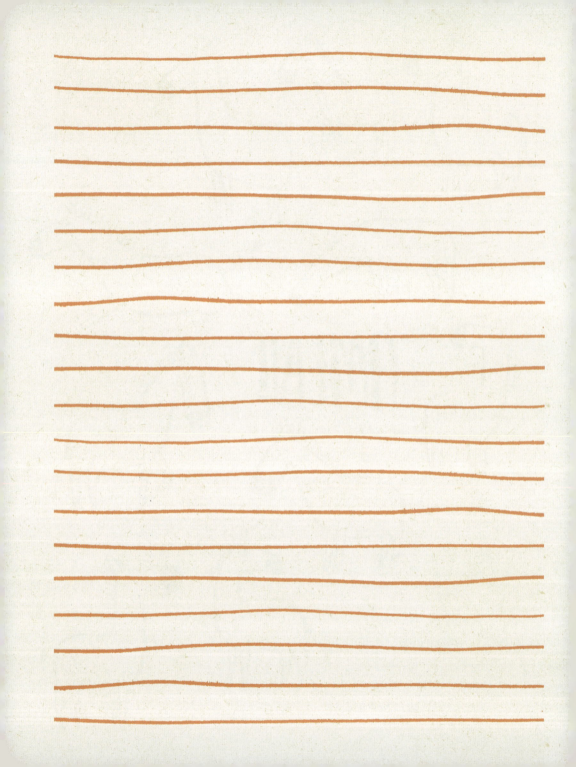

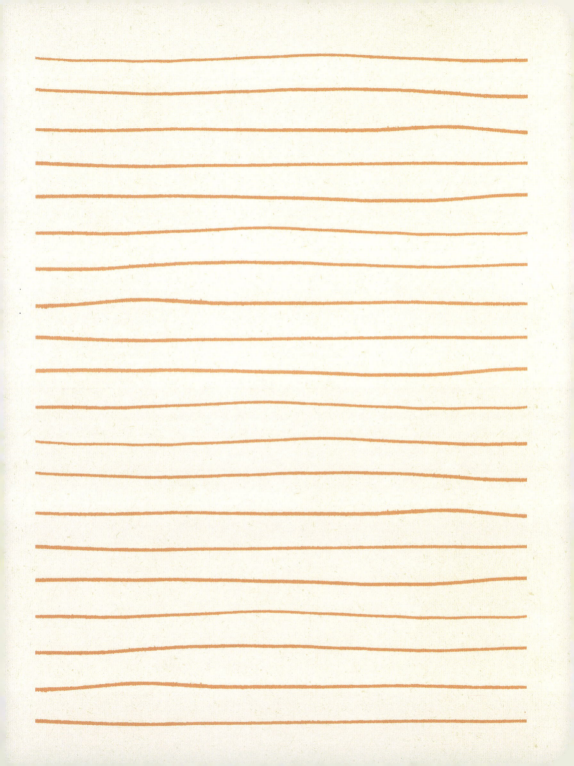

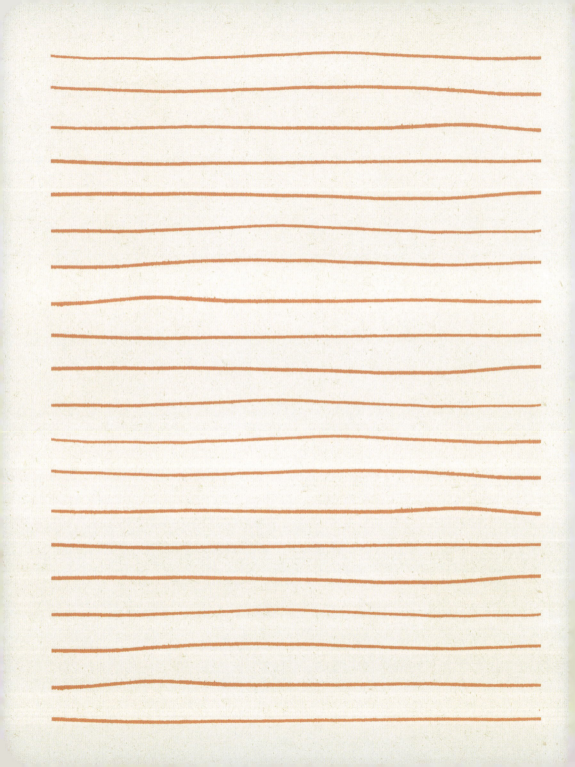